OUT OF → THIS WORLD

VIRGINIA LOH-HAGAN

ANTIMATTER

45TH PARALLEL PRESS

Published in the United States of America
by Cherry Lake Publishing
Ann Arbor, Michigan
www.cherrylakepublishing.com

Reading Adviser: Marla Conn, MS, Ed.,
  Literacy specialist, Read-Ability, Inc.
Book Designer: Jessica Rogner

Photo Credits: © Color4260/Shutterstock, cover, 1; © John Fowler/
  Flickr, 5; © sakkmesterke/Flickr, 7; © Designua/Shutterstock, 8;
  © Seo Ilyoung/Shutterstock, 11; © Hanna_photo/Shutterstock, 12;
  © Belish/Shutterstock, 15, 23; Carl D. Anderson/WikiMedia/
  Public Domain, 16; © Eliyahu Yosef Parypa/Shutterstock, 19;
  © CERN PhotoLab/WikiMedia, 21; © anttoniart/Shutterstock, 25;
  Unknown author/WikiMedia, 27; © Smithsonian Institution/Flickr, 29
Graphic Element Credits: © Trigubova Irina/Shutterstock

45th Parallel Press is an imprint of
Cherry Lake Publishing Group

Library of Congress Cataloging-in-Publication Data
Names: Loh-Hagan, Virginia, author. | Loh-Hagan, Virginia.
  Out of this world.
Title: Antimatter / by Virginia Loh-Hagan.
Description: Ann Arbor, Michigan : Cherry Lake Publishing, 2020 |
  Series: Out of this world | Includes bibliographical references
  and index.
Identifiers: LCCN 2020006897 (print) | LCCN 2020006898 (ebook) |
  ISBN 9781534169234 (hardcover) | ISBN 9781534170919 (paperback) |
  ISBN 9781534172753 (pdf) | ISBN 9781534174597 (ebook)
Subjects: LCSH: Antimatter-Juvenile literature.
Classification: LCC QC173.36 .L65 2020 (print) | LCC QC173.36 (ebook) |
  DDC 530-dc23
LC record available at https://lccn.loc.gov/2020006897
LC ebook record available at https://lccn.loc.gov/2020006898

Printed in the United States of America | Corporate Graphics

TABLE OF CONTENTS

WHAT IS THE UNIVERSE?

The universe is huge. It's everything that exists. This includes planets, stars, and outer space. It includes living things on Earth.

The universe contains billions of galaxies. Galaxies are huge space collections. Galaxies are made up of billions of stars, gas, and dust. Galaxies include **solar** systems. Solar means sun. Earth is in the Milky Way galaxy. Galaxies spin in space. They spin very fast. There's a lot of space between stars and galaxies. This space is filled with dust, light, heat, and rays.

Before the birth of the universe, there was no time, space, or matter. Anything that takes up space is matter. Matter can exist in different states. The common states include solid, liquid, and gas. This is why things like air and smoke are considered matter. But the heat and light from a fire aren't matter. These don't take up space.

The universe hasn't always been the same size. It also hasn't always existed. Some scientists believe it began with a "big bang."

The Milky Way is very old.

This is a **theory**. Theory means an idea. This theory explains how the universe was born. First, the universe was a super tiny blob, smaller than a pinhead! Then, that super tiny blob exploded. This happened 13.8 billion years ago. Next, energy spread out. Energy is made from matter. For example, the flames in a fire are matter. They take up space. But the heat you feel and the light you see from the flames are energy. Last, stars and planets formed. This all happened in less than a second.

Scientists think the universe is still expanding. Expanding means growing or spreading out. Scientists also think this expanding process is speeding up.

CHAPTER ONE

WHAT IS ANTIMATTER?

"Anti" means against or opposite. An antidote is something you give someone to stop poison. You use antibacterial soap to stop bad bacteria from spreading. Does this mean that antimatter is the opposite of matter? Yes! Antimatter has the opposite properties of normal matter. Properties are qualities or traits.

Matter is all around us. It's made up of atoms. There are different types of atoms. These are called elements. Oxygen is an element. Water is an element. When atoms get together, they create particles. Atoms consist of protons and electrons. Protons help make up the center of an atom. The center of an atom is called the nucleus. Electrons orbit the nucleus. Electrons and protons have an electric charge. This is what gives them energy. Electrons have a negative charge. Protons have a positive charge.

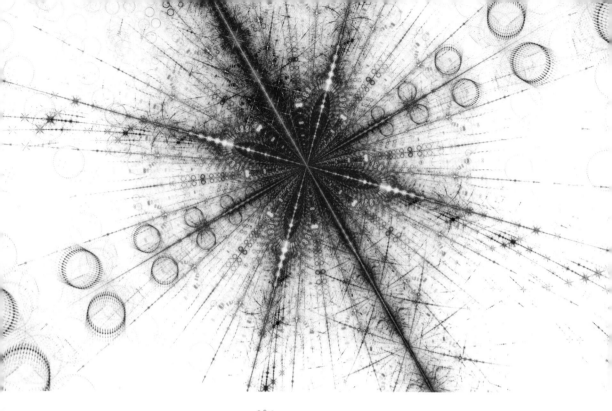

Antimatter particles are created in super high-speed crashes.

Antimatter is the opposite. It consists of antiprotons and antielectrons, also called positrons. Antiprotons and positrons are similar to protons and electrons. Antiprotons help make up the center of an antimatter atom. The center of an antimatter atom is called an antinucleus. Positrons orbit the antinucleus. Positrons and antiprotons also have electric charges. They're the opposite of electrons and protons. Positrons have a positive charge. Antiprotons have a negative charge.

After the big bang, only energy existed. Things cooled. They expanded. Particles and antiparticles were created. Particles are little bits of matter. Antiparticles are little bits of antimatter.

Matter and antimatter were made at the same time. Some scientists think the same amounts were made. Other scientists think more matter was made than antimatter. This explains why matter is all around us. It also explains why antimatter is rare. Scientists don't know why yet. Antimatter is still a mystery. It's still being studied.

 Each element has a certain number of electrons, protons, and neutrons.

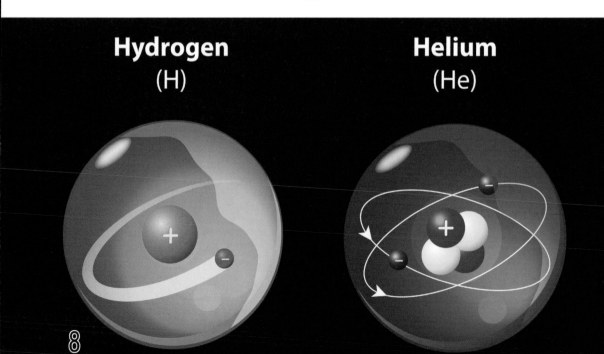

Hydrogen
(H)

Helium
(He)

AMONG THE STARS:
WOMEN IN SCIENCE

Dr. Fabiola Gianotti is a trained ballerina. She also plays piano. She was drawn to science. From a young age, she loved nature. She was inspired by her father. Her father studied rocks. She was also inspired by Marie Curie. She got a doctorate in experimental particle physics. She's the first female director-general of CERN. CERN is the European Organization for Nuclear Research. Gianotti said, "I hope that my being a woman can be useful as an encouragement to girls and young women who would like to do fundamental research but might hesitate ... They have similar opportunities as their male colleagues." Gianotti has been celebrated as a top scientist. She's written over 650 science articles. She said, "There are many [questions]: the composition of dark matter, the origin of the matter/antimatter asymmetry in the universe. We will continue to work and hopefully we will be able to solve, at least partially, some of these issues."

CHAPTER TWO

WHERE CAN ANTIMATTER BE FOUND?

Most matter can be seen and felt. Antimatter is a different type of matter. It hasn't really been proven. But there are strong signs that antimatter exists. Scientists found evidence in space. They did this using special calculations. Calculations are math problems.

Small amounts of antimatter constantly rain down on Earth. They come in the form of **cosmic rays**. Cosmic rays are energy particles. They're fast. They travel from space at high energies. Tiny amounts of positrons are found in these particles.

Antimatter is found in the remains of big, dead stars. These remains are called **pulsars**. Pulsars spin at fast speeds. They have powerful **magnetic fields**. These fields have electrons and positrons.

 Pulsars have been called the "lighthouses of space."

Scientists found antimatter in lightning. Lightning is a flash of light. It's caused by the discharge of electricity. It has **gamma rays**. Gamma rays are the highest energy form of light. They react with air. This reaction makes positrons.

There's evidence of antimatter in bananas! They release a positron once every 75 minutes. Bananas are considered **radioactive**. Radioactive means emitting energy. But don't worry! Bananas are safe to eat.

Scientists have made antimatter. They've tested it. When antimatter and matter meet, they destroy each other. This crash creates huge amounts of energy. Scientists think they can use antimatter to power spaceships. But man-made antimatter doesn't last long. Scientists are trying to solve this.

 Some scientists make machines using bananas as an energy source.

DOWN-TO-EARTH EXPERIMENT

Want to see how electric charges work? Try this experiment. Learn how positive and negative charges attract each other. Learn how charges that are the same repel each other. Think like a space scientist!

Materials:

- 2 balloons
- Sweater
- Water

Instructions:

1. Blow up both balloons.

2. Hold 1 balloon next to the other balloon. Nothing happens. The balloons are neutral. They have no charge.

3. Rub the balloons on your sweater. This adds electrons to the balloons. It causes the balloons to be negatively charged.

4. Rub the balloons in your hair. Positively charged hair attracts to negatively charged balloons. Hair rises up to meet the balloons.

5. Hold the balloons next to each other again. Like charges repel. The 2 balloons repel each other. Opposite charges attract.

6. Rub 1 balloon on your hair. Bring the balloon close to running water. Water starts off neutral. The charged balloon pushes electrons away. This leaves a positively charged area.

CHAPTER → THREE

HOW CAN ANTIMATTER BE STUDIED?

It's hard to study antimatter. Matter is all over. This means antimatter can easily be destroyed. Scientists must stop this from happening. They have to trap antimatter. They must do this for a short period of time. They do this in Penning traps.

Penning traps are **devices**. Devices are tools or machines. They're made for a specific purpose. Penning traps hold charged particles. They hold positrons and antiprotons. Penning traps are like tiny **accelerators**. Accelerators are machines that speed things up. Inside Penning traps, particles move around. Magnetic and electric fields keep them from crashing.

Small amounts of antimatter can be created inside of particle accelerators.

Hydrogen is the simplest element. It's easy to study. It's easy to understand. This is why scientists create and study **antihydrogen**. Antihydrogen is the antimatter equivalent to hydrogen. Antihydrogens have positrons and antiprotons. They're neutral particles. Neutral particles can't be trapped by electric fields.

Scientists found that Penning traps don't work on certain antihydrogens. So they use special traps. These traps create an area of space. In this space, the magnetic field gets larger. It gets larger in all directions. Neutral particles get stuck in the area with the weakest magnetic field.

By trapping antimatter, scientists can study how it works. They can do experiments. There's so much scientists don't know about antimatter. They have more questions than answers.

 Antihydrogen was the first antimatter made by scientists. This was in 1995.

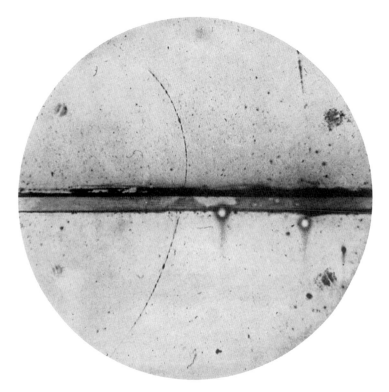

IT'S (ALMOST) ROCKET SCIENCE

At CERN, scientists study antimatter. They want to see how matter and antimatter act. They want to compare them. They need to make antimatter in order to study it. They use an Antiproton Decelerator (AD). Decelerators are machines that slow things down. The AD is the only machine of its kind. It's very special. A proton beam is fired into a metal block. Antiprotons are created. They have too much energy. They move in different directions. They move at different speeds. The AD tames the particles. It slows them down. It turns them into a low-energy beam. This beam can be controlled. It's used to make antimatter. The AD is a ring. It has magnets. The magnets keep the antiprotons on the same track. Strong electric fields slow them down. Antiprotons cool down. Then, they slow down. This happens several times. Finally, the antiprotons become ready for study.

CHAPTER FOUR

WHAT ARE THE CHALLENGES WITH ANTIMATTER?

Antimatter is powerful. A handful of antimatter makes a lot of power. Some people want to use it as an energy source. They want to use it as **fuel**. Fuel is gas. It powers machines. Some people want to use it to make weapons. A gram of antimatter could make a big explosion. The explosion could be the size of a **nuclear bomb**. Nuclear bombs are the result of the splitting or colliding of atoms. To do any of this, large amounts of antimatter would be needed. But antimatter is hard to make. It's hard to find. It's hard to store.

 The U.S. Air Force funded military studies that used antimatter in the Cold War.

Scientists can make small amounts of antimatter to study. They don't have the technology to **mass-produce** it. Mass-produce means to make large amounts. Scientists can hold small amounts in traps.

But they can only do this long enough to study it. They can't hold it long enough to use it. There's no technology that could store antimatter for long periods of time.

Creating and storing antimatter is expensive. It would cost $100 billion to create 1 milligram of antimatter. There are 1,000 milligrams in 1 gram (0.04 ounces). The average paper clip weighs about 1 gram (0.04 ounces). That's super tiny! Antimatter is the most expensive substance on Earth. It's also the rarest.

Scientists at CERN use special machines to study antimatter.

21

CHAPTER FIVE

HOW IS ANTIMATTER USED IN MEDICINE?

Antimatter is used in medicine. A PET scan is a test. It examines the chemical activity in the body. It shows how tissues and organs are working. It detects sicknesses. Flourine-18 is sent into the bloodstream. This is done with drugs or needles. Flourine-18 goes to areas in the body that use a lot of energy. It goes to problem areas. It emits positrons. Positrons meet electrons in the body. They destroy each other. This makes gamma rays. The rays let the PET machine take pictures. PET is a special machine. It lets doctors see things that other machines can't. (The "P" in PET is positron.)

Scientists are working on using antimatter to treat **cancer**. Cancer is a sickness. It occurs when cells go out of control. It causes **tumors**. Tumors are growths. These growths aren't normal. They spread. They kill cells in the body. They can cause death.

Doctors rely on machines to help their patients.

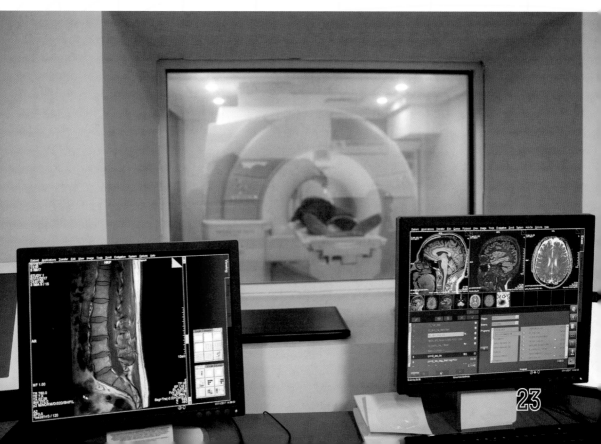

Doctors target tumors. They use beams of proton particles. Doctors kill bad cells this way. Scientists think antiprotons could be better at killing cancer cells. They're working on the Antiproton Cell Experiment (ACE). They're testing antiprotons. Antiproton beams have 4 times more energy. Scientists are working on focusing the energy better. They don't want to damage healthy cells.

 Antimatter is also found in our bodies!

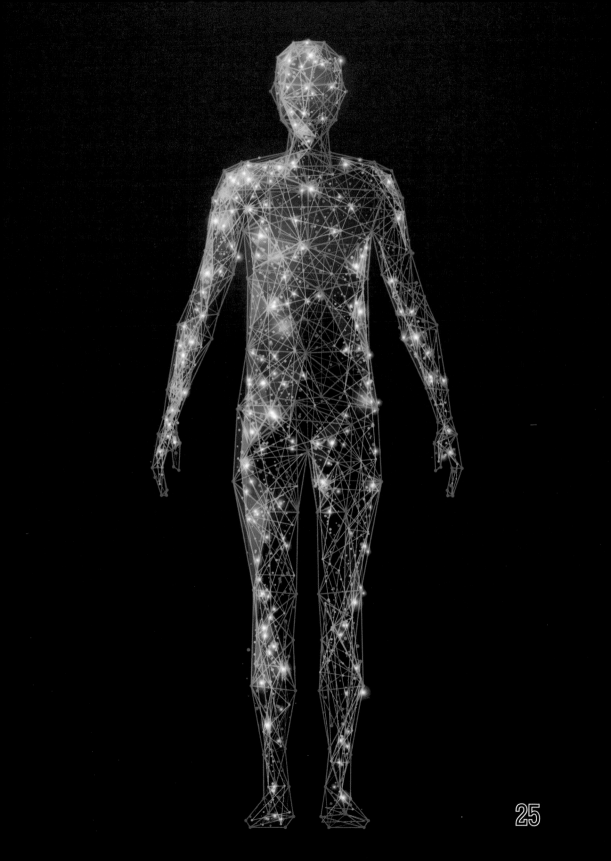

25

CHAPTER → SIX

WHO FIRST STUDIED ANTIMATTER?

Dr. Paul Dirac lived from 1902 to 1984. He was a British scientist. He studied electrical engineering and math. In 1928, he was studying the movement of an electron. The electron was traveling near the speed of light. Dirac created an **equation** to describe this. Equations are math statements. Scientists use equations to explain things. Dirac showed that for every particle, there was an antiparticle. He also showed that the antiparticle matched the particle with an opposite charge. Dirac's equation won him a Nobel Prize. It opened possibilities for the study of antimatter. It was the first time something never seen was predicted to exist.

Dirac based his work on Albert Einstein's theory of relativity.

In 1932, Dr. Carl Anderson proved Dirac's equation. He studied physics and engineering. He lived from 1905 to 1991. He discovered the positron. He won the Nobel Prize in 1936.

He was the first to see particles in cosmic rays. He studied pictures. He saw a weird curve in the cosmic ray paths. He thought the particles caused the curve. He said the particles had the same mass as electrons. He said the electrons had opposite charges. He called these positive electrons "positrons." He was the first to identify an antiparticle.

 Anderson was an American scientist.

29

ACCELERATORS (ak-SEL-uh-rate-urz) machines that speed things up

ANTIHYDROGEN (an-ti-HYE-druh-juhn) neutral particle that has positrons and antiprotons

CANCER (KAN-sur) a sickness caused by abnormal growth of cells and tumors

COSMIC RAYS (KAHZ-mik RAYZ) fast energy particles that travel from space

DEVICES (dih-VISE-iz) tools or machines that are made for a specific purpose

EQUATION (ih-KWAY-zhuhn) mathematical statement used to explain how things are equal

FUEL (FYOO-uhl) gas

GAMMA RAYS (GAM-uh RAYZ) highest energy form of light

MAGNETIC FIELDS (mag-NET-ik FEELDZ) areas that have moving electric charges

MASS-PRODUCE (mas-pruh-DOOS) to make large amounts

NUCLEAR BOMB (NOO-klee-ur BAHM) bomb made as the result of splitting atoms

PULSARS (PUHL-sarz) the remnants of massive dead stars

RADIOACTIVE (ray-dee-oh-AK-tiv) emitting energy

SOLAR (SOH-lur) relating to the sun

THEORY (THEER-ee) an idea meant to explain something

TUMORS (TOO-murz) abnormal growths that kill cells in the body

- Antimatter exists in the Van Allen Belts. These radiation belts are around Earth. They're zones of charged particles. They include antiprotons. Particles come from solar winds and cosmic rays. They're held by Earth's magnetic field. The belts are thought to be the most abundant sources of antiprotons near the Earth.

- So far, scientists have made enough antimatter to power a lightbulb for 3 minutes. They can hold antimatter for 16 minutes. If all the antimatter made by man was destroyed at once, the energy would be weak. It wouldn't be enough to boil a cup of tea.

LEARN MORE

Pohlen, Jerome. *Albert Einstein and Relativity for Kids: His Life and Ideas with 21 Activities and Thought Experiments.* Chicago, IL: Chicago Review Press, 2012.

Tyson, Neil deGrasse. *StarTalk: Everything You Ever Need to Know About Space Travel, Sci-Fi, the Human Race, the Universe, and Beyond.* Washington, DC: National Geographic, 2017.

Tyson, Neil deGrasse, with Gregory Mone. *Astrophysics for Young People in a Hurry.* New York, NY: Norton Young Readers, 2019.

ABOUT THE AUTHOR

Dr. Virginia Loh-Hagan is an author, university professor, and former classroom teacher. She's excited about the uses of antimatter in science fiction. She lives in San Diego with her very tall husband and very naughty dogs. To learn more about her, visit www.virginialoh.com.